More Lunch Bag Notes

Also from Loyola Press:

**Lunch Bag Notes: Everyday Advice
from a Dad to His Daughter**

Ann Marie Parisi and Al Parisi

More Lunch Bag Notes

Anthony Parisi
& Al Parisi

Everyday Advice
from a Dad
to His Son

LOYOLAPRESS.

CHICAGO

LOYOLAPRESS.
3441 N. ASHLAND AVENUE
CHICAGO, ILLINOIS 60657
(800) 621-1008
WWW.LOYOLABOOKS.ORG

Cover and interior design by Adam Moroschan

Library of Congress Cataloging-in-Publication Data
Parisi, Anthony.
  More lunch bag notes : everyday advice from a dad to his son / Anthony
Parisi & Al Parisi.
      p. cm.
  Includes index.
  ISBN 0-8294-2171-8
  1. Fathers and sons—Religious aspects—Christianity. 2. Sons—Religious life.
I. Parisi, Al. II. Title.
BV4529.17.P37 2005
248.8'32—dc22
                                                        2005004371

Printed in the United States of America
05 06 07 08 09 10 Bang 10 9 8 7 6 5 4 3 2 1

Introduction

Some five years ago, during my sister Ann Marie's sophomore year at Agoura High School in Agoura Hills, California, our dad, Al Parisi, started writing notes on her brown-paper lunch bags. They were wonderful notes full of wisdom and good advice. Dad's notes were meant to inspire Ann Marie and her friends to believe in themselves and make sound moral choices in their lives. Unbeknownst to Dad, my sister saved his notes so that she could one day share them with her children. She flattened out each lunch bag and stored them in a sneaker box for safekeeping.

About four years ago, Ann Marie was cleaning out her closet, and the box fell off the shelf and bonked her on the head. The box opened up and the lunch bags went scattering all over the bedroom floor. When she told Dad what had happened, he laughed hysterically, then became very quiet, realizing that Ann Marie thought the notes precious enough to save them. You could see he was extremely touched.

As chronicled in Ann Marie's edition of *Lunch Bag Notes,* the notes were eventually self-published so their wisdom could be shared with local teens and their parents. The books were mostly distributed through fund-raisers at our alma mater, Agoura High School, and at local parishes. Many books were simply gifted. Ann Marie's goal was to get the messages out to as many local teens and their parents as possible, and to grow spiritually and mentally from the experience. However, when Ann Marie and Dad realized the positive impact the book was having on its readers, they choose to go the next step and seek out a Catholic publisher to help spread the message to a much broader audience. Loyola Press was that publisher.

Next it was my turn. In my sophomore year at Agoura High School, Dad wrote notes of love and wisdom to me, just as he had to Ann Marie. However, I warned Dad early on that if he was going to write me lunch notes, he had better not write them on my lunch bag, but rather on a separate piece of paper placed *in* the bag. Those notes, unedited except for grammar and spelling, follow. I hope you enjoy reading them, and that they inspire you as much as they inspired me.

—Anthony Parisi

How to Use This Book

Since you, like most readers, will find that you have experienced situations similar to the ones addressed in the notes—or likely will encounter them—each note is accompanied by a journal page containing a brief comment to stimulate your thought process. We recommend that you use these pages to record your feelings and emotions, or anything else that comes to mind after reading the accompanying note. Usually your first thoughts will be the strongest and the ones that are most meaningful. By taking time to write out your thoughts, you will be more likely to understand how you can apply the note to your own life experience. For instance, you may feel conflicted about a decision, choice, or action that you need to take. Ben Franklin, whenever he was faced with a crucial decision, would write out each possible choice on a separate piece of paper, and then draw a line down the middle of each page. On one side he would write potential positive outcomes of his decision; on the other, the potential negative outcomes. When finished, he would opt for the choice with the most potential for a positive result. Like most good decision makers, he took his time deciding, but once he did, he was firm in his commitment.

The right-hand pages are lined for your convenience. For easy reference, at the bottom right of each journal page, you will also find the theme(s) of the accompanying note.

More Lunch Bag Notes

Dear Anthony,

Summer school was a good choice, though I know a difficult one for you. Nearly half your summer vacation seems like a lot to give up! Now, however, I am sure you're glad you did because you maintained very good grades, despite all the time you devoted to the Agoura High School baseball team. Good job.

Love, Dad

2

Do you have difficulty seeing beyond the present? When have you sought instant gratification? When have you planned for the future? Seeking only instant gratification has its consequences. Most virtuosos require a minimum of eight years of "investing in themselves" before they attain true accomplishment and fame. When necessary, give up short-term gains or gratification, and invest in your future. Don't worry about what you might have to give up, but rather, think about what you will *gain*. Plan to succeed by succeeding to plan. . . . More on that later.

{ **Choices** }

Dear Anthony,

As you begin your sophomore year, you can build on the experience of last year. As a freshman you had several concerns: the huge campus, bigger classes, the pressure of playing baseball and basketball while maintaining good grades, and making new friends.

What you discovered is that every other student has the same or similar concerns, and that there is no magic formula for "fitting in" and adjusting. All you can do is be yourself.

Love, Dad

When have you tried to be someone else in order to fit in? What happened? Be true to yourself and be yourself, and soon you will fit in. Shakespeare made a career of writing plays about hapless characters who tried to be what they were not. The plays are called *tragedies*. You are unique; why be a "copy"? Stand tall and be proud.

{ **Self-Confidence** }

Dear Anthony,

You flatter me when you say you want to be a success like me. Let me tell you some of the things I did in high school that enabled me to succeed later on in life:

* I listened intently in class and took very good notes.

* Every week, sometimes every day, I rewrote the notes from the lessons of that day while they were still fresh in my mind.

* I did every extra-credit project.

* I spread out my studying, but really focused on the evening before an exam.

* I got at least eight hours of sleep every night.

Love, Dad

Are your grades good? What is your system for studying and doing well on tests? If your grades aren't very good, it may be because you haven't developed the system just right for you. Resolve to do so *now* and avoid regrets. The longer you go without a plan or system, the more difficult it will be to study well in the future. Make a checklist of the tasks described in the note, and track your progress every day.

Dear Anthony,

You're beginning to make a lot of girl friends. That's good, but there are ground rules that apply to girls that you don't necessarily need to pay attention to with boys. Call it "Girl Etiquette":

* Be yourself and don't create an alter ego.

* Always be respectful.

* Always be complimentary.

* Do not tease a girl or make fun of her in any way. (Of course, this same rule applies to your guy friends.)

* "Don't touch." Unfortunately, in today's society, <u>touching</u> is taboo.

Love, Dad

Do you have a problem with any of these ground rules or are any of them difficult for you to follow? Why or why not? If you cannot follow these rules, you may be headed down a dangerous path. Chivalry is not dead. It's every woman's wish to be treated as a lady. Be a gentleman and your popularity with women will soar.

{ Dating }

Dear Anthony,

I know you think Mom and I are hounding you when we ask a lot of questions about your friends. The questions we ask show our genuine concern and love for you. They are also the same questions you should be asking yourself.

Friendship is a special gift. You can't give it to everyone, nor can you accept it from everyone.

The good news is that we do approve of those friends that we have met.

Love, Dad

How do you choose your friends? What do you know about them? Remember this old adage: "Show me your friends, and I will tell you what you are." The true test of friendship is knowing that your friend will stand by your side in good times and in bad.

_____

_____

_____

_____

_____

_____

_____

_____

_____

_____

_____

_____

_____

_____

_____

_____

_____

_____

_____

{ **Friendship** }

Dear Anthony,

Jack Nicklaus, the famous golfer once said: "I never hit a shot, not even in practice, without having a very sharp, in-focus picture of it in my head."

The key phrase in this saying is "in-focus." This does not only apply to sports, but also to all aspects of life. In order to do something well, we need to focus. That is why I often say to you: "<u>Age quod agis</u>," which means, "Do what you are doing." In other words, avoid distraction and concentrate. Anything worth doing is worth doing well.

Love, Dad

Do you have difficulty concentrating? Why or why not? What are the distractions in your life? To properly focus, try doing one thing at a time so that you can do it well. Try to find a quiet place where you can avoid distractions. If the place is your room, make sure the TV and CD player are off.

{ **Success, Studying** }

Dear Anthony,

I notice you are getting more frequent quizzes and exams than last year, so I thought I would remind you of some good test-taking techniques:

* Be prepared by studying well; avoid surprises.

* Get eight to ten hours of sleep.

* Have a healthy breakfast.

* Before beginning the exam, take a deep breath and relax; remind yourself that you will do well because you are well prepared.

* Read the instructions well.

Love, Dad

Have you made adjustments to your study habits? What have they been? Keep trying new studying techniques until you find the method that works best for you. Be self-correcting. You may be surprised by how much your grades improve. Remember the checklist and find a "quiet place" to study.

{ **Studying** }

Dear Anthony,

A follow-up to yesterday's note—
particularly on why it's important to read
the instructions: Once, when I was involved
in a math competition, I started the
exam from the back. It was such an easy
test that I finished before anyone else.
Eventually, when I reached the first page
and briefly glanced at the instructions,
my pulse began to quicken as I realized
why the test was so easy: It was to be
done in base five.

Love, Dad

When have you not followed instructions because you thought you knew what you were doing? What happened? It is a good idea to follow instructions, especially those from parents, teachers, and coaches. They really do know best. Imagine you asked for directions to a particular event and all you remembered was that it was ten miles away. How would you find it?

{ **Success** }

Dear Anthony,

I really appreciate your help whenever we have to assemble something or change a timer. I know I couldn't do it without you. [Dad has difficulty processing new information as a result of a brain tumor he had some years ago.] It's nice of you to take the time to help me. Sometimes I wish we had more of these kinds of projects to do, just so we could be together. And thank you for going easy on me with your teasing.

Love, Dad

When have you teased others who had disabilities? When have you avoided people who are handicapped? Try to see Jesus in everyone. Look beyond the disability. Many disabled people have been pillars of our society: Franklin Delano Roosevelt, Helen Keller, Christopher Reeve, Les Brown, to name but a few. (Brown, labeled "educable mentally retarded," is one of today's most highly acclaimed speakers. He talks to *Fortune* 500 companies and conducts seminars throughout the United States.) Remember Jesus' compassion toward the lepers, those tormented by demons, and all the infirm.

{ **Respect** }

Dear Anthony,

You are blessed with a loving and caring family. We love you for so many reasons. Here are just a few:

* You are kind and considerate.

* You make us laugh.

* You make time for everyone, especially little kids. Your patience with them is remarkable. That is very special.

* You're willing to help out other people when they ask, like Donna and Mr. Carmichael, even though you could be hanging out with your friends.

* You have a great smile, laugh, and sense of silliness.

Keep being you.

Love, Dad

How do you spend quality time with your family? How do you help others? Your presence and your time are great gifts to give. Sir Winston Churchill once said: "We make a living by what we get, we make a life by what we give." The more you give of yourself, the better you'll feel about yourself.

{ **Family, Stewardship** }

Dear Anthony,

Have you heard this saying: "If it feels good, just do it"? It doesn't make any sense, unless we add the clause, "Provided it's morally correct." Our forefathers, especially Thomas Jefferson, noted that freedom is not freedom if it interferes with the freedom or rights of others.

To do something simply because it feels good, without considering its consequences or whether it's morally right, is terribly wrong. We must always consider the ramifications of our actions.

Love, Dad

What do you do just because it feels good? When have you acted without thinking about the consequences of your action? Recall what happened to Adam and Eve when they chose to act impulsively. Doing the right thing is easier than you think. You already know what's right and what's wrong. To paraphrase basketball coach Pat Riley: Pick the right one, then go with it.

{ **Character, Choices** }

Dear Anthony,

You've had a good attitude lately. To have a great attitude is even better. As I often shared with Ann Marie, attitude pretty much determines how far you will go in life. Very few people, including me, have been successful without having a positive attitude. You always say you want to be like me. Remember to always be SMART. [That's my dad's acronym for Superior Mental Attitude Results in Triumph.]

Love, Dad

How is your attitude? Do you see the glass as half-empty or half-full? With a positive attitude, you can and will do things better. What is it like to be around people with a negative attitude? How does it affect you? Negativity can be contagious; avoid contact with it. Our thoughts steer our minds to fulfill them. Therefore, as Peter Pan advised: "Think happy thoughts."

{ Attitude }

Dear Anthony,

The other day you indicated you'd like to try something new, like joining a school club. That's a great idea. The more active we are in life, the more fulfilling life is. Yes, our minds, our bodies, even our souls, all need exercising. Work hard, play hard, and pray hard.

Love, Dad

Are you a participant or an observer? Mental exercise, physical exercise, and spiritual exercise keep us strong. Don't be a couch potato. What positive and fun activities can you participate in? Do them now. If you hesitate, you may change your mind. Remember what Confucius said: "The journey of a thousand miles starts with but a single step."

{ Action }

Dear Anthony,

One of the things I admire most about you is your modesty. You are always quick to credit others for your success, and you readily accept responsibility for your mistakes or shortcomings. Did you know that these are two of the most important traits of a leader?

Love, Dad

When have you accepted responsibility for your mistakes? When have you blamed others? When have you bragged too much about yourself? Always be humble in victory or defeat, and you'll be well on your way to becoming a leader. Leaders accept responsibility and lead by example. Choose to be a leader.

{ **Responsibility** }

Dear Anthony,

St. Paul said, "so we, who are many, are one body in Christ, and individually we are members one of another" (Romans 12:5 NRSV). He then pointed out that each of us is blessed with unique gifts from God, which we are to share with one another—this is called stewardship.

Anthony, you should determine what talents you have and how you can best use them. Unlike natural resources, if we do not use our talents, they wither away.

Love, Dad

What are your talents? Make a list of your best qualities and traits (good listener, helpful, make time for others, athletic, musically talented, patient, etc.). This will help you determine your talents. Now, how can you be a good steward and use your talents for the betterment of others? Serving others will help you improve your self-esteem, strengthen your character, and lead you to happiness.

{ **Stewardship** }

Dear Anthony,

In a previous lunch note I mentioned how powerful our minds are. For example, many prisoners grew up frequently hearing the words: "You will end up in jail someday." Many professional athletes were told: "Someday you'll play in the major leagues." I am not a clinician, but it seems to me that the way things turn out is the result of more than mere coincidence.

I urge you to fill your mind with positive input by reading good books, by watching good movies, and by reminding yourself daily that you are a good person and that God loves you.

Love, Dad

How do you feed your mind? Our minds are like computers: If you input positive thoughts, you'll get positive results. If you input negative thoughts, you may export negative results. What can you do to better feed your mind? You could read a good book, watch an uplifting movie, listen to a beautiful song or motivational audiotape, explore an enriching computer program, or simply think positive thoughts and/or affirmations.

{ Attitude }

Dear Anthony,

The U.S. Constitution doesn't guarantee us happiness, only the pursuit of it. What delights me is that you're always pursuing happiness and at the same time remembering to do your chores. Should I or anyone else not compliment you today, remember to give yourself a compliment—that is what Mark Twain would say.

Love, Dad

What are you doing to pursue happiness? What else could you do that would make you happy? Wholesome activity is one way of pursuing happiness. A reminder, again: Do not be a couch potato. Begin a new activity today. Don't hesitate or you may fall back into the same old rut. Find a hobby or join a school club. *Just do it!*

{ **Action, Happiness** }

Dear Anthony,

St. Padre Pio of Pietrelcina, a recently canonized Italian saint, to whom the Nonni [Italian for "grandparents"] and I have a great devotion, never doubted God's divine assistance. Don't despair over the calamities that surround you because everything will turn out for God's glory and the salvation of souls. In other words, God only allows bad things to happen to us—and sometimes denies us the lesser pleasure of good—in order to lead us to the greater good of spiritual and moral growth.

Love, Dad

How do you handle disappointment? Have you endured any suffering? If so, how did you handle it? If not, why do you feel that you have never suffered?

Always rely on the Lord. He is there with you, both in bad times and in good times. Get yourself a copy of the famous poem, "Footprints." Let go of your frustrations and sorrows by offering them up for the souls in purgatory.

{ **Failure** }

Dear Anthony,

Character is what defines us long after we are gone. Always remember to protect your reputation by being honest and trustworthy. Never let anyone pressure you into doing what you know should not be done. When in doubt remember: WWJD (_W_hat _W_ould _J_esus _D_o).

Love, Dad

What peer pressure are you experiencing from your friends or from others? A true friend would not suggest you do something morally wrong, would he? Perhaps it is time to reevaluate who your real friends are. Friendship is a precious gift; be careful to whom you give it and from whom you receive it.

{ Friendship }

Dear Anthony,

Pope John Paul II said: "It is not wrong to live better; what is wrong is a lifestyle that presumes 'having' is better than 'being.'" It is a poignant message. It reminds us of our stewardship role; that is, we must be willing to share our time and treasure with those less fortunate. As Mom always says, happiness is wanting what you have, not having what you want.

Love, Dad

What "things" do you always desire? Things may make us happy in the moment, but hardly ever in the long run. Try helping out someone in need of your time or your talents. Is there an elderly person you know whom you can simply visit for a brief time or perform some chores for on a regular basis? Isn't that what God expects of you? These are the "things" that bring us long-term happiness—even eternal happiness.

{ **Stewardship, Happiness** }

Dear Anthony,

You have much to be thankful for. Always show your appreciation, especially to God. Father Dave once told me: "If you aren't thankful, God may stop sending his blessings."

Love, Dad

When have you recently thanked someone for a kind act or a gift? When have you thanked God? Do you remember to thank God for all his blessings? It is a very nice gesture to send a thank-you note whenever you receive a gift. It takes only a few minutes, but it reaffirms for the person who gave you the gift that you were deserving of it.

{ Gratitude }

Dear Anthony,

In order to make future profits, corporations as well as individuals make investments. The best investment I know is the <u>investment</u> you can make in yourself! This investment requires no money, but it does require your time and effort. If you remain focused and work hard, you'll get to play hard.

Success for companies, sports teams, and individuals must be "earned." I know no other way, nor do I know any shortcuts.

Be SMART!

Love, Dad

What efforts have you made toward self-improvement? A little effort every day can pay big dividends in the long-term. One example might be to learn the meaning and proper usage of one new word every day—before you know it, your vocabulary, your writing, and your speech will improve tremendously. Just one word a day; it's that easy.

{ Success }

Dear Anthony,

St. Paul tells us "we are the temple of the living God" (2 Corinthians 6:16 NRSV), and that "the Spirit of God dwells in you" (Romans 8:9 NRSV). This is an awesome privilege and responsibility. Now that you're beginning to go to more parties, you might encounter some other teens who might be drinking, smoking, or taking drugs. They are obviously unaware that they are polluting their bodies and the temple of God.

If you see that type of activity going on, I trust you would do the right thing and leave the party. It may be difficult, but you know it is the right thing to do. At any gathering, especially if there are people you do not know, never let your drinking glass out of your sight.

Love, Dad

What temptations do you face? How are you keeping your mind and your body pure? Are you reading, watching, or playing anything that could be polluting your mind or body? Do you realize the awesome privilege and responsibility you have? How are you responding?

{ Character }

Dear Anthony,

Worry causes tension and can be debilitating. Worry cannot solve the issue we are worried about; only action can. Worrying about the past and the future is futile. Live today to the fullest, and tomorrow will be an even better day.

Be proactive and remember to "smell the roses."

Love, Dad

What do you worry about? Have any of your past worries proved to be needless? We cannot change the past, and we cannot predict the future; we can only deal with the present. If we do a good job with the present, the future will take care of itself. In the words of the prophet Isaiah: "Behold, God is my salvation; I will trust, and will not be afraid." (Is 12:2 KJV)

{ **Failure** }

Dear Anthony,

St. Augustine commented on how man marvels at the beauty of nature, yet when he sees his own reflection in the water, he fails to recognize the beauty of God's greatest creation: man himself. God told us in the first book of the Bible, Genesis, that he created us in his own image; therefore, it stands to reason we would be his best work. God does not make junk.

If we all remembered that we are each created in God's image, wouldn't life be grand? Love and peace would supplant hatred and war. Remember to always see God in others.

Love, Dad

When do you see God in others? When do you appreciate the beauty of nature? When do you see the beauty in you? If you look closely enough, you will see Jesus in the homeless, the homebound, the sick, the wealthy, and the strong. Look up into a clear sky some night and ponder the awesome beauty of creation. Look always with the eye of faith.

{ Respect }

Dear Anthony,

Judy Garland, world-famous singer and actress and the star of <u>The Wizard of Oz,</u> said: "Always be a first-rate version of yourself, instead of a second-rate version of someone else." This is another reminder to always be true to yourself and be the best you can be.

Enjoy your weekend. Be thankful and show it! Make us proud.

Love, Dad

When have you put on a different persona to impress others? Why did you do it? Sometimes people don't act like themselves because they have low self-esteem. If you believe that God is in you, why would you want to be someone else? Behave as if you believe in yourself, and others will sense your self-confidence. Then you will indeed develop a stronger sense of self.

{ **Self-Confidence** }

Dear Anthony,

Get ready for Brooklyn, Son. Make everyone feel your love. Spend time catching up with everyone, and share with them what's going on in your life. Listen attentively so that people know that you do care about what they have to say.

Love, Dad

How are you sharing quality time with your family? Do you listen attentively or listen with your own agenda? How do you share what's going on in your life with your family? Good communication with family members is integral to keeping the family together. If you don't know what's going on in the lives of your family members and they don't know what's going on in your life, how can you be supportive of one another?

{ Family }

Dear Anthony,

St. Francis de Sales said: "The love of God and the love of one another should be the basis of our entire way of life."

St. Francis saw cheerfulness and cordiality as ways of expressing our love for God. He also said patience with others, and with ourselves, was extremely important—even more important than fasting.

Love, Dad

How do you express your love for others? What else could you do to show love? When we express our love for others we also express our love for God. Show God you love him by loving others. Have you told your sibling(s) or your parents "I love you" lately? Do so often and your relationships will grow stronger and stronger. Persist in doing so, even if they don't say "I love you" back.

{ **Family, Friendship, Respect** }

Dear Anthony,

We love how you take time for everyone, especially the little kids around us, like David, Luca, and Julia Rose.

Remember that today is the Feast of the Immaculate Conception. This holy day of obligation celebrates the fact that our Blessed Mother is the only human person to be born without the stain of original sin. God our Father gave her this grace so that she could be the mother of his Son, our Lord and Savior, Jesus Christ.

Love, Dad

For whom do you take time in your life? How do you act when you are with them? Don't you enjoy being around people who are happy and cheerful? If you want people to flock to you, doesn't it make sense for you to be happy and cheerful? What is it that cheers you up? Is it a great book, participating in sports, being with friends and family? Chances are that it's all these and a lot more. The point is, it is difficult to be happy and content if you only spend time by yourself.

{ **Happiness, Character** }

Dear Anthony,

In this week of finals, remember the saying: "_Age quod agis_," which, if you recall, means, "Do what you are doing." In other words, remain focused and avoid distractions. The three most important things you can do this week are study, study, and study. If you prepare well, you're likely to do well—wouldn't you agree?

Love, Dad

When are you able to "do what you are doing"? Are you able to do it with your schoolwork? When you are not "present" while doing something, it is difficult for you to do it well. Do you have poor study habits and still expect to receive good grades? This is one of those rare opportunities when you can control the outcome. This is your opportunity to be a prophet.

{ **Studying** }

Dear Anthony,

Remember: First encounters and your education (and nearly everything you do) are done in one take. Life is not a rehearsal; there are no do-overs. <u>Seize the day!</u>

Love, Dad

How do you give your best effort to make a good first impression? Do people have a good impression of you when they meet you, or do you have difficulty putting your best foot forward? First impressions are normally lasting impressions; it is difficult to overcome a poor first impression. This is a lesson that you will learn over and over again as you go through life. Resolve to make a good first impression and to attempt to do all things well from the outset.

{ Attitude }

Dear Anthony,

I have one favor to ask you. I know you think it's funny to act like a smart aleck, and sometimes it is. Very often, however, it is disrespectful.

When I ask you for a little space and some quiet, please honor my request, as I do yours.

Love, Dad

Have you ever hurt your parents' feelings or made them angry when you were just trying to be funny or have some fun? When? It is important to honor and respect your parents. Having a sense of humor is a wonderful and healthy thing, but remember: There is a time and place for everything. Before you say something, you should always consider how the other person(s) might take it.

{ **Respect** }

Dear Anthony,

Whatever you dream about achieving, you can probably do so with a positive attitude. It is highly unlikely that with a negative attitude you can make any dream come true. Accomplishing a goal takes time, patience, determination, and persistence. Remind yourself often that, just like "the little engine that could," you _can_.

Make a plan and work the plan. Determine how you'll handle obstacles. Should you fail, remind yourself that failure is simply the path to success.

Love, Dad

What do you daydream about doing? Do you believe you can make your dreams come true? If your answer is yes, you probably can. If your answer is no, you probably can't. There are many wonderful, easy-to-read motivational books available in the library, and many are also available on tape. If you would like some specific recommendations, contact us. [See page 229.]

{ **Success** }

Dear Anthony,

I am so proud of you for the way you accept defeat on the playing field and for your humility in victory. I also like the way you look for new challenges. It reminds me of one of my favorite sayings from Will Rogers: "Why not go out on the limb? That's where the fruit is."

Love, Dad

How do you handle victory and defeat? Do you allow the disappointment of defeat to linger? Be gracious in defeat and remember tomorrow is another day. Vince Lombardi said, "If you can't accept losing, you can't win."

Have you ever taunted your opponent(s) in victory? Victory and defeat are both common elements of life. They each help determine our character, and character is how people see us. Sportsmanship applies not only on the field but in all aspects of life.

{ **Failure, Success** }

Dear Anthony,

A parent can have no greater joy than to be told by another adult how wonderful his child is. I had this experience twice last week. First, on Sunday, I met your teachers, who told me you are a wonderful young man. Then, on Monday, Father Bill said that you were remarkable on the retreat—"a chip off the old block."

Thank you for bringing Mom and me so much joy.

Love, Dad

How do you try to make your parents proud? It is one of the greatest gifts you can give to your parents. You can make your parents proud by being the best you can be at all times. It's that simple. Have you written down on paper your plan of action for improving your life and the lives of those around you? Have you hung some pictures on your wall and your mirror to remind you of your plan?

{ **Family, Success** }

Dear Anthony,

Live a Christ-centered life. Use WWJD as your guide. This, my son, is the path to true happiness. Things may provide happiness for a short while, but eventually you need more and more things to maintain happiness. Having Jesus as the center of your life provides for eternal happiness here on earth, and ultimately, in heaven.

Love, Dad

Are you still looking for the "thing" that will make you happy? What do you think it is? Invite the Lord to be your daily companion. If you do so, you will develop an inner peace, an inner happiness, that no material objects can bring you. You may want to find a private place, away from distractions, where you can have a dialogue with Jesus daily. Remember to start your day greeting the Lord and inviting him to join you in your day's activities.

{ Faith }

Dear Anthony,

Abraham Lincoln once said: "You have to do your own growing no matter how tall your grandfather was." It's an interesting use of words isn't it?

Naturally, "growing" refers to one's maturity. We develop our own maturity. It is not inherited the way our height is. We mature by learning from life's experiences; therefore, no endeavor is a waste of time if we learn from it.

Love, Dad

74

Do you sometimes think an activity, like a homework assignment or a family chore you're asked to do, is a waste of time? Why or why not? It is only a waste of time if you don't do it cheerfully and try your hardest. Anything you do is worth doing well, isn't it? We never know how some "trivial" thing we do will impact our future, but whether in the short or long term, it somehow does. For instance, think about a current circumstance in your life and backtrack the sequence of events that led to it. It's likely that even a small change in the entire sequence would have yielded a different result.

{ **Character** }

Dear Anthony,

I have noticed that your homework assignments are getting heavier and more complicated. It is important that you keep pace. Procrastination is the worst of all possible choices. No one has ever procrastinated their way to the top. Be SMART!

Love, Dad

What have you put off until tomorrow that you could have completed today? Is this becoming a regular occurrence? Procrastination can be habit-forming, and you should do everything you can to avoid it. It's simple: Resolve now to do all projects, small or large, on time. Timeliness is an extremely important habit, especially when you are in the working world. Be SMART and start making timeliness a habit.

{ **Responsibility** }

Dear Anthony,

With Christmas quickly approaching,
I want to remind you of the obvious:
Jesus is the reason for the season. The
wonderful tradition of giving presents
brings us joy, as it did for the Magi, who
presented the infant Jesus with wonderful
presents. If done properly, the giving of a
gift should bring us greater joy than the
receiving of a gift.

Your presence in my life is a wonderful
present. I love you very much, Son.

Love, Dad

What is the proper Christmas spirit? Do you have it? Why or why not? With the countless commercials and advertisements we see on TV and in magazines and newspapers, it can be difficult at times to remember that Jesus is, in fact, the reason for the season.

Do you want to experience a great joy? Give a present to someone who doesn't expect it.

{ **Faith, Gratitude** }

Dear Anthony,

As I once told Ann Marie, two of my favorite Christmas activities are decorating the house and watching our favorite Christmas movies together as a family. I relish the time we spend together. It is the greatest gift you can give me.

Love, Dad

Are you spending quality time with your family? What activities can you do together during the holidays? Why not make your presence the gift that you give to your family?

Dear Anthony,

Don't get too uptight about what you want to be when you grow up. Life is hard enough as it is. Worrying about your future just makes things more difficult.

For now, I suggest that you focus on your short-term and intermediate goals. I'm glad to see that you've written out what those goals are, and even hung pictures on your wall and mirror to remind you.

In a few years you can begin to modify your goals as your options become clearer.

Love, Dad

hat are your goals? What are your worries about the future? Resolve to live in the present. The future is still a mystery for all of us. You can best provide for your future by doing whatever you do well. What positive action can you take today to build a stronger tomorrow? Brainstorm. This is important if you want to discern your goals and begin a regimen to bring them to fruition.

{ **Attitude, Success** }

Dear Anthony,

Success is 80 percent attitude and 20 percent aptitude (intelligence).

In other words, all the knowledge in the world doesn't guarantee you success. Nothing guarantees success, but we can put the odds greatly in our favor by being persistent and forging ahead despite any obstacles encountered.

Love, Dad

Have you set a goal for yourself and then given up at the first difficulty? Why did you give up? Don't go it alone; find a mentor. Read books on positive attitude; you'll find many in your public library.

{ **Attitude** }

Dear Anthony,

Here are some examples of people who pressed on despite hardships, criticism, threats, etc.:

* Nearly all the signers of the Declaration of Independence died penniless, and the British killed many of them, along with their families.

* Abraham Lincoln, poor and without formal education, became the sixteenth president of the United States—and that was the first election he ever won.

* Most of all, we have the example of the apostles, who, despite knowing that they would be persecuted and probably killed for proclaiming and spreading the faith, nevertheless pressed on with heroic virtue.

Love, Dad

What difficulties have you overcome in order to accomplish a goal? How did it feel? If you can't think of an example when you have persevered, it is time to experience one. Are you ready for your next challenge? Sure you are—and when you conquer that challenge you'll be hungry for the next.

{ **Success** }

Dear Anthony,

January is named after Janus, the Roman god of good beginnings and happy endings.

Start the year off by remembering each and every morning, before you even get out of bed, to thank God for the gift of a new day. Proclaim: "Lord, let's make it a great day together." At the end of each day when you go to bed, again give thanks to God and proclaim, "Thank you, Lord, for this great day."

Love, Dad

How do you make God an essential part of your day? When you do so, have you noticed an improvement in how you live each day? If you don't do something to share each day with God, why don't you? What better partner is there than Jesus himself?

{ Faith }

Dear Anthony,

There is an old expression: "He who hesitates is lost." It refers, of course, to the opportunities that we do not take advantage of—<u>missed</u> opportunities. Be bold and aggressively grasp every opportunity that comes your way. Don't procrastinate because, if you do, the opportunity may disappear. A good baseball analogy would be: "You miss all the pitches you don't swing at."

Love, Dad

Do you feel you miss out on opportunities? Why or why not? Have you let opportunities pass you by? Remember: Rarely does an opportunity come around twice. What will you do the next time opportunity knocks on your door? Answer it!

{ **Success** }

Dear Anthony,

At this point in your life, you really haven't had too many difficult decisions to make. The few you have had, Ann Marie, Mom, and I have been there to give you advice and counsel.

There will be many times in the near and distant future when you will need to make quick decisions. The simplest way to ensure that you are choosing wisely is to consider: What Would Jesus Do? You will discover that sometimes the right decision is the most difficult one. That is why it helps to have Jesus as your guide.

Love, Dad

What good choices have you made? What poor choices have you made? Have you consulted with others when you were not sure what decision to make? With whom? When your parents, or an elder, are unavailable and you need to make an on-the-spot decision, rely on our Lord to help you make the right choice.

_____

_____

_____

_____

_____

_____

_____

_____

_____

_____

_____

_____

_____

_____

_____

_____

{ **Choices** }

Dear Anthony,

Always remember that "service of and witness to our faith" is a necessary requirement for salvation. St. James, in his epistle, reminds us that faith without works is dead.

Jesus affirms the scribe who tells him that in order to achieve salvation we must love God with all our strength, with all our mind, and with all our heart; and that we must treat others as we would want them to treat us. That is the Golden Rule.

Love, Dad

How do you witness to the faith? How do you treat others? A more important question might be: How do you treat those who have no way to repay you? It's easier to treat kindly those who can do something for you, isn't it? You may want to assist a person in need or perhaps mentor a young child.

{ Faith }

Dear Anthony,

I am sorry that the "relationship" with your girlfriend ended so abruptly. I know you really liked her.

At your age, this is not only common but healthy. Dating should be fun, and probably best experienced in a group. Don't put pressure on yourself to have a "relationship."

Enjoy meeting and dating new girls. Eventually you'll know what type of woman you want to have a true relationship with.

Love, Dad

Are your dating experiences fun? Why or why not? Are you trying too hard to find a girlfriend? Are you being yourself or are you putting on a persona? Dating should be natural and fun, not pressure-filled.

{ Dating }

Dear Anthony,

Sometimes we are hurt by those closest to us. Even Jesus was betrayed by one of his own apostles.

Most of us have experienced hurt, me included. Though it is difficult to forgive and forget in these circumstances, you seem to handle it very well. It is very admirable that you could so easily obey Jesus' command to forgive our neighbor.

Love, Dad

Do you have difficulty forgiving others? Why or why not? If you are unable to forgive others, how can you expect the Lord to forgive you? Some of the best relationships develop when forgiveness is extended to another. Is there anyone needing your forgiveness? Keep in mind that forgiveness doesn't require you to become best friends with the person you have forgiven. Does that make forgiveness easier for you?

{ **Forgiveness** }

Dear Anthony,

One of the best things you can say about people is that their word is their bond. Based on how some of our politicians, business leaders, and sports heroes act at times, being trustworthy would seem to be unimportant.

Don't be fooled by bad examples. Once they're found out, those who have abused the trust of others find it very difficult to regain that trust, and eventually, they become ostracized.

You know that I trust you.

Love, Dad

When was your word your bond? When have you broken your word to someone? Do you say what you mean and mean what you say? Trust is too important a virtue to lose, so protect it.

You have probably read or heard about executives who did not keep their word. Had they known the shame and hurt they and their families would experience, they might have chosen to be honest and thus retain the trust of those most important to them. What do you think?

Dear Anthony,

I am sorry that you're not enjoying the second year of confirmation as much as the first. You had a remarkably good team leader last year, didn't you?

If your team leader is not as strong this year, perhaps you can help him by privately offering some thoughts on how to make the ninety minutes more interesting and stimulating.

Make sure you are part of the solution and not part of the problem.

Love, Dad

What do you do when you find a teacher uninteresting? Have you ever made suggestions on improving performance to an adult? How did the adult respond? Not all teachers, preachers, or even parents are good communicators. Nevertheless, you can't use that as an excuse to space out. If you have thoughts on how to improve things, express yourself either by talking to the person or writing a note if that makes you more comfortable. Isn't it worth putting forth the effort to have a positive experience?

{ **Communication** }

Dear Anthony,

Have you ever noticed that when you don't take Mom's or my advice, things seem to go wrong? Like yesterday, when you refused to take a sweatshirt or jacket to school, and you came home sick.

The suggestions we make are for your well-being. Why else would we make them? Unless it is a life or death situation, we allow you to make your own choice, hoping you will learn from experience, as we all have.

Love, Dad

When have you rejected your parents' advice and counsel? Why did you do so? Were you being rebellious? Do you do this routinely? Do you think your parents would ever knowingly give you bad advice? If you think they may be wrong, don't be argumentative. Instead, discuss the issue civilly. This will show your parents you are mature and respectful, and will help you earn their trust—and their respect.

{ **Family** }

Dear Anthony,

I am sorry that you're disappointed about not having a swimming pool. I am, too, but unfortunately we don't have the room for even a small pool.

Dwelling on that fact does neither of us any good. Focus on what you do have: a wonderful family, a beautiful home, a gorgeous garden, a spa, a gym, and a playroom.

Be SMART!

Love, Dad

What are the biggest disappointments that you have faced? Do you dwell on disappointments or do you focus on all the good in your life? There is probably far more good in your life than you realize. Look for it. Remember, too, that happiness is wanting what you have, not having what you want.

{ **Failure, Happiness** }

Dear Anthony,

You are very good about saying thank you. I would suggest that whenever possible you also send a handwritten thank-you note. Sending a note tells the person that you really care.

When I was in business I made a habit of sending at least five handwritten notes out each day. I developed very strong relationships with vendors and clients alike. I only wish I would have started the habit sooner.

My inspiration for doing this was St. Francis of Assisi. I had read he was a prolific letter writer and that many of his letters are still in existence.

Love, Dad

Whom can you thank today? To whom can you write a note today? Write a note of thanks to your parents, your sister or brother, your aunt or uncle, or a friend you haven't seen for a while. There is always great pleasure in receiving a note, letter or a card—especially when it's unexpected. Make someone happy today by sending a note. Don't know what to say? A simple, "I was thinking of you," is all you need to say.

{ **Gratitude** }

Dear Anthony,

There are 86,400 seconds in every day. How do you choose to use them? Remember, a millionaire, a sports star, a doctor, and a lawyer each has the same number of seconds in any given day.

It's what you <u>do</u> with those seconds that counts.

Be SMART!

Love, Dad

How do you use your time? Do you use it wisely or do you waste it? Success does not come from watching the clock, but rather, from ignoring it. Work hard, play hard, pray hard, and love hard. That's the path to happiness.

{ **Success** }

Dear Anthony,

Happiness is fleeting if we seek only instant gratification or ego-centered happiness (personal power and control).

Long-term gratification is achieved by going beyond ourselves; that is, living a life pleasing to God. We can best do this by loving our neighbor.

Love, Dad

Who comes first in your life? If it's you, then your happiness will only be short-term. If it's God, your family, your friends—and then yourself—happiness will last forever.

{ **Happiness** }

Dear Anthony,

Our ultimate goal is heaven. All our activity should be directed toward achieving this ultimate goal. Under no circumstances should we ever do anything that we think might lead us off the "path of perfection."

However, we all make mistakes, and hopefully, we learn from them. That is what the sacrament of penance is all about. We resolve to do our best to avoid making the same mistake again and to return to the right path.

Love, Dad

What are the biggest mistakes that you have made? Do you let your failures overwhelm you? Resolve to learn from your mistakes and failures, and try to avoid them in the future. Frequently receive the sacrament of penance.

{ Faith, Failure }

Dear Anthony,

Little-known St. Cunibert, who lived and died in the seventh century, is an excellent role model for you. As a teen, he was obedient, patient, prayerful, pure, generous, and trustworthy.

The king took notice of him, adopted him as a son, and arranged for his education. Imitate the virtuousness of this young saint and you, too, will stand out from the crowd.

Love, Dad

How do you display the qualities of the teenage St. Cunibert? Try each day, each week, or each month to develop one of St. Cunibert's virtues: obedience, patience, prayer, purity, generosity, and trustworthiness. By doing so, you will become a good role model for others and someone who stands out because of his character.

{ **Character** }

Dear Anthony,

Nelson Mandela, the South African leader, said, "The greatest glory in living lies not in never failing, but in rising every time we fall."

Sir Winston Churchill, England's prime minister during World War II, said, "Success is going from failure to failure without loss of enthusiasm."

These are words of wisdom.

Be SMART!

Love, Dad

What failures have you experienced that eventually led to success? Is it becoming clearer to you that failure is the path to success? There are few success stories that aren't preceded by stories of trial and error.

Dear Anthony,

Every now and then life deals us a bad hand. Instead of complaining about it (a useless activity that changes nothing), focus on your attitude and play the hand as best you can.

No one has, or will ever have, a life without some disappointment. That would be called heaven.

Love, Dad

When have you been dealt a bad hand? What do you do with it? Do you complain when things don't go exactly as you plan? You cannot control the circumstances in your life, but you can adjust your attitude toward them. Make an attitude adjustment and play your hand as best you can.

{ **Failure, Attitude** }

Dear Anthony,

I enjoy your company very much. I never had that opportunity with <u>Nonno</u> (Italian for Grandpa) because he was an immigrant and didn't speak the language well or understand our culture.

Nonno missed out on all my sports and scholastic achievements. I resolved long ago to make sure I didn't miss out on yours. My favorite time together with you was our father/son trip to the Baseball Hall of Fame in Cooperstown, New York, last summer.

Love, Dad

What was your favorite time spent with your dad? Do you make a sincere effort to spend quality time with him now? Find an activity that you can share with your father and ask him to join you in it. You may be surprised by how much both of you enjoy your time together.

Dear Anthony,

One of my favorite issues to discuss is character. I know I've told you before, but it's worth repeating: Character is what defines us. It is difficult to imagine someone rising to the top without strong character; it's even more difficult to imagine someone remaining on top without it.

Love, Dad

How have you been working to improve your character and people's perception of you? What steps have you taken? Are they working? If not, make adjustments, not wholesale changes.

{ Character }

Dear Anthony,

A follow-up on yesterday's note about character: Here are some snippets from famous people:

"If you don't have enemies, you don't have character."

—Paul Newman
actor and humanitarian

"If you think about what you ought to do for other people, your character will take care of itself."

—Woodrow Wilson
president of the United States

"The best index to a person's character is how he treats people who can't do him any good."

—Abigail Van Buren
("Dear Abby")

Love, Dad

These quotes come from people with irrefutable character. How can you emulate them?

_____

_____

_____

_____

_____

_____

_____

_____

_____

_____

_____

_____

_____

_____

_____

_____

_____

_____

_____

{ **Character** }

Dear Anthony,

People love your smile. I bet you don't even realize how much your smile can do for someone.

Keep smiling.

Love, Dad

When have you brightened someone's day with a smile? When has someone brightened yours? Focus on smiling all day and you'll feel better about yourself. You also will brighten someone else's day.

Dear Anthony,

I thought I would share with you some ideas on dating:

* Explore the girl's likes and dislikes. Listen attentively.

* You learn more about her by asking questions than by talking about yourself. It also shows interest when you ask thoughtful questions.

* Use e-mail. It is easier sometimes to discuss in writing issues that might otherwise be more difficult or uncomfortable in person.

* Be yourself. Don't gossip about others. Be complimentary when appropriate.

Love, Dad

What do you think of these ideas? What do you think would happen if you tried all of these with a girl you are dating?

If you're not yet dating, it's no big deal. The suggestions—especially about listening attentively—apply whenever we are engaged in any relationship.

_____

_____

_____

_____

_____

_____

_____

_____

_____

_____

_____

_____

_____

_____

_____

_____

_____

_____

_____

{ **Communication, Dating** }

Dear Anthony,

The great humanitarian physician Albert Schweitzer said: "The first step in the evolution of ethics is a sense of solidarity with other human beings." (Ethics make up our belief system and help us decide what is moral or immoral.)

Do not be fooled by those who seem to get away with cheating, lying, and scamming. The media are full of their sad stories. In the end they all get caught, and they and their families suffer shame.

Remember: WWJD.

Be SMART!

Love, Dad

I t may sometimes be difficult to do the "right" thing, but consider it the "only" thing to do. Do you have a "sense of solidarity with other human beings"? What have you done that reflects this idea?

{ **Character** }

Dear Anthony,

The book of Proverbs has this advice for young adults: "Remember the Lord in everything you do, and he will show you the right way" (Proverbs 3:6 TEV).

Once you have determined the right way, stand firm in your decision.

Love, Dad

When did God show you the right way? When did you end up taking the wrong way? By now you should be pretty good at making decisions. Are you? If not, why not? Remember to make choices based on logic, not emotions. Sometimes it's better to let a day go by if the situation is too emotional.

{ **Character, Choices** }

Dear Anthony,

I am very impressed with your workout habits. I do want to caution you, however, about parading in front of the mirror too much. You see, that takes you from being genuinely proud of your physique to being vain, and vanity can be sinful.

Be SMART!

Love, Dad

How do you feel about your body and the way you look? When have you shown vanity? It's good to look your best; after all, our bodies are the temple of the Holy Spirit. Just try to avoid excess.

{ **Self-Confidence** }

Dear Anthony,

Have you noticed that every few months one of the family cars goes in for routine or preventative maintenance? The reason we service cars is so they won't break down. Similarly, if we don't service our body with good food and exercise, it breaks down. If we don't service our soul with prayer, piety, service to others, and the Eucharist, then our relationship with God breaks down.

Love, Dad

How do you service your body? How do you service your soul? Are you using the proper fuels for your mind, body, and soul? Keep up the maintenance, and you'll retain your value, just like a fine-tuned automobile.

{ Faith }

Dear Anthony,

I am so proud of you and the other second-year candidates for confirmation. Cooking and serving dinner for the senior citizens of our community is a wonderful expression of love and an essential part of stewardship.

Great job.

Love, Dad

Have you ever experienced the joy of serving the elderly or helping your grandparents? What was it like? The look in their eyes is itself a reward, but it is also our way of giving back to God.

{ **Stewardship** }

Dear Anthony,

Enjoy your upcoming retreat. It will be a unique experience for you. I have been to the Benedictine abbey where your retreat is being held. The monks are wonderful. Walking the hills of the monastery is a transcendental experience. I urge you to walk the hills and experience the quiet. You can feel God's presence in the gentle breeze.

Love, Dad

When have you had a powerful experience in nature? Why did it affect you the way it did?

Have you had the opportunity to go on a spiritual retreat? If not, inquire at your parish office. It could be a life-changing experience.

{ Faith }

Dear Anthony,

A thought on prayer and faith today:

When you pray for something, act as if you have already received it. In other words, if you ask God for courage, be brave; if you ask for patience, be patient; and if you ask for wisdom, be wise.

Love, Dad

44

How is your prayer life? What do you pray for? Do you petition God for favors and then sit around waiting for your prayers to be answered? That would be like praying for an A on an exam and then not studying, wouldn't it?

{ **Faith, Prayer** }

Dear Anthony,

Albert Camus, the Nobel Prize–winning French novelist/playwright, wrote: "Life is the sum of all your choices."

Doesn't that sound familiar? It's similar to what I tell you often: "People are where they are because they choose to be there." If we find ourselves at the wrong place in life, there's no blaming others. We are, after all, free to choose well or poorly.

Be SMART!

Love, Dad

Are you disappointed with where you are? Why or why not? Tomorrow, the first day of the rest of your life, start to make choices that will get you to where you want to be. To assist you in making wise life-changing choices, take a sheet of paper and draw a line down the middle. Write down your possible choices and deduce the possible positive and negative outcomes. Choose the option that has the best chance to produce a positive result. This is called the Ben Franklin Method because it was the technique he used.

{ **Choices** }

Dear Anthony,

I'm very pleased with the patience you're showing in learning how to drive.

Driving is not a right; it's a privilege. An automobile is like a loaded weapon, especially if it isn't taken seriously by its driver and passengers. I know you are aware that teens have been involved in several tragic, even fatal, accidents in our neighborhood. That is why Mom, Ann Marie, and I are strict about making certain you concentrate at all times. The number one reason for accidents is distraction.

Be SMART!

Love, Dad

Do you pay attention every moment you are driving? What can distract you from the road in front of you and the other cars around you? Oftentimes it's other passengers.

Whether or not you have begun to drive with a license or permit, you should pay attention whenever you are in a car. Do you? The slightest distraction can result in tragedy—and the phone call no parent ever wants to receive.

{ **Responsibility** }

Dear Anthony,

I'm so happy to hear you say that you will pass on basketball this season in order to concentrate on getting higher grades. It is a wise and mature decision.

Love, Dad

When do you feel overwhelmed? Is your plate too full? If you stretch yourself too thin, it becomes difficult to do all things well. Try to prioritize. Which would you prefer, to be good at only a few things or average at many things? Think about it before answering.

{ **Priorities** }

Dear Anthony,

I'm glad you're taking my advice and going to a Spanish-language tutor. I know it's taking away from some of your free time, but it is the right thing to do; otherwise, you may fall too far behind and never recover. I like the way you are prioritizing. It's a sign of wisdom and maturity.

Love, Dad

How have you prioritized your schoolwork and activities? Perhaps you are having difficulty doing so. Try this: List all your activities down the left side of a piece of paper and rate them according to the importance they have in your life. Rearrange them from most important to least important. If you find you're too busy, you may want to cut back on those items that are least important.

{ **Priorities** }

Dear Anthony,

One of the most important traits you can have is self-confidence. Self-confident people are leaders and inventors. They establish the paths to progress. Self-confidence inspires you to be your best.

Here are some steps to help you develop a strong level of self-confidence:

* Remember that God created you, and God doesn't make any junk.

* Jesus commanded us to love God, our neighbors, and ourselves. This implies self-respect, which leads to self-confidence.

* Have a positive attitude and act as if you've already accomplished what you set out to achieve.

* Be patient and deal with obstacles. Let nothing deter you.

* Remind yourself daily that your goals are good and wholesome.

Love, Dad

How is your self-confidence? If it is not at a healthy level, seek advice and counsel from God, your parents, and others whom you trust. Begin working on your self-confidence immediately. Don't delay. You can start by making a list of all your good qualities. Yes, another list—but putting it together is worth the time and effort you'll spend on it.

{ **Self-Confidence** }

Dear Anthony,

Long-term happiness is achieved by going beyond our "self." What that means is: We must live a life full of justice, love, and stewardship. Being good must be an end in itself. All our decisions must be focused on the greater good.

Eternal happiness includes doing all of the above for the love of God.

Love, Dad

How do you live a life full of justice, love, and stewardship? When do you desire only immediate gratification? It is certainly easier to achieve than long-term happiness, but is that what life is all about? The good news is that you can achieve immediate gratification *and* long-term happiness. How do you think you can do that? Another list may help you figure it out.

{ **Happiness** }

Dear Anthony,

I know you remember to say good morning to the Lord every day and good night to him when you go to sleep. But how about the rest of the day? Acknowledge his presence throughout the day. Short and simple prayers are fine. Speak to him as you would speak to any friend and listen closely—you might hear something very profound that you would not hear from any other friend.

Since prayer is a dialogue with the Lord, it requires you to listen. Don't you agree?

Love, Dad

How is your prayer life? Do you remember to walk and talk with Jesus daily? When would be a good time for you to pray each day? Is it on your way to school, walking around campus, or perhaps on your way home? "Hi, Jesus; thanks for being by my side," is a simple but powerful prayer.

{ Prayer }

Dear Anthony,

As I've told you, our ethics instruct us on proper behavior, reminding us to do what we should do in any circumstance. Being ethical sometimes requires that we don't do what we want to do. That can often put us in conflict with our peers. Ethics require you to be strong and courageous.

Being ethical allows you to look in the mirror and be proud of the person you see. If you're ethical in all you do, you will never have to look over your shoulder or have a guilty conscience.

Be SMART!

Love, Dad

What do you feel peer pressure to do that you know you should not do? Be bold and courageous, and always be true to yourself. Every morning and every evening you have to look at yourself in the mirror; someday you will have to look directly at God. Remember to rely on WWJD. Recall the earlier references to those corporate executives who were unethical and remember what happened to them.

{ **Character, Choices** }

Dear Anthony,

You have been in the second half of your sophomore year for a while now, and I'm noticing how much you have improved in time management. You're doing very well handling school, sports, social activities, and confirmation classes. You have, however, been a little lax in keeping your room tidy, an activity that might only require an additional five minutes a day.

If you would please manage to do that every day, Mom and I would really appreciate it.

Love, Dad

How do you manage your time? Are you good at time management? Why or why not? Perhaps you haven't begun to prioritize yet. The irony is that, if you take the time to do so, you will actually create more time for yourself. Why not use your journal and do so now?

{ Priorities }

Dear Anthony,

A few reminders on how to live a life pleasing to God:

* See Jesus in everyone.

* Be compassionate and forgiving.

* Be a good steward.

* Maintain a good sense of humor.

* Don't go it alone—remember, WWJD.

Love, Dad

How are you living a life pleasing to God? Do you find it difficult or easy to do? It can be easier if you remember to act ethically, become a good steward, and remain God-centered. This is one area where you are in complete control. No one can interfere in your relationship with the Lord.

{ Faith }

Dear Anthony,

The Jewish Talmud states: "It is fitting for a great God to forgive great sinners." Jesus said we are to forgive others as he forgives us. In other words, if we do not offer forgiveness to those who hurt us, how can we expect Jesus to forgive us when we hurt him?

Be SMART!

Love, Dad

When someone hurts you, do you hold a grudge? Why or why not? What do you expect to get out of holding a grudge? It will only make the hurt linger. Nothing but true forgiveness can free us from the hurt. Sounds like another opportunity to write a note to someone needing your forgiveness, doesn't it?

{ **Forgiveness** }

Dear Anthony,

As an athlete, I thought you would appreciate learning about an organization called Life Athletes.

Their brochure states: "Life Athletes is a coalition of over two hundred professional and Olympic athletes committed to leading lives of virtue, abstinence, and respect for life." Its members are committed to living a life pleasing to God by always doing the right thing, even when it's difficult (sound familiar?); saving themselves for the special person they marry; respecting the lives of others, especially the unborn and the aged; and by never quitting or making excuses for failure. Wow!

Be SMART!

Love, Dad

There is a lot of good stuff here. Challenge yourself to be like a Life Athlete. What are some things that you could do to emulate the Life Athlete credo?

Dear Anthony,

Lent is a time to grow closer to God by doing extra acts of kindness, as well as by fasting and praying. Make a great Lent. It is more important than having a great game or great season, isn't it?

Love, Dad

n what ways can you grow closer to Jesus Christ, our Lord? Remember: He never moves away from us. Perhaps this Lenten season you can focus on doing special things for those in need. That is more important than giving up chocolate or ice cream.

{ Faith }

Dear Anthony,

One measure of having had a good Lent is, if at the end of the forty days, you can truly say: "I feel closer to my Lord and Savior Jesus Christ."

Though it is customary to give up favorite things for Lent, it is far more holy to do <u>good works</u>.

Love, Dad

What things can you do to make it a good Lent for you? You may want to consider helping an elderly relative or friend, mentoring a youngster, visiting someone who is sick, or working in a soup kitchen.

Dear Anthony,

I understand that you've been invited to a dance by one of the girls at Agoura High School. That's wonderful.

Remember to be a gentleman and pay complete attention to her, and not be distracted by your friends. Compliment her, dance with her, talk with her; and at the end of the evening, remember to thank her.

And be SMART!

Love, Dad

Dating should be a part of your youth. It should be a fun, wholesome experience for you and the girl, especially if you respect each other. What are some ways that you can be a better date and make the experience memorable for both of you?

{ Dating }

Dear Anthony,

Friends sometimes disappoint us. It is important not to judge them too harshly or too quickly, and not to act out of disappointment. Be careful not to inflame the situation. It's an explanation and reconciliation you want, right? Naturally that does not mean to capitulate, but it does mean to be ready to forgive and forget. A good friendship is worth saving, isn't it?

Love, Dad

When has a friend hurt you? Did you react hastily or did you take the time to determine how you could save the relationship (assuming of course it's worth saving)? Regardless of whether we save the relationship, we must always be ready to forgive and forget, as our Lord Jesus instructs us.

Dear Anthony,

I have suggested to you to always be Christlike by doing what Jesus would do. Jesus never spoke half-truths, only the absolute truth. Yes, he is God and therefore perfect and unable to lie or deceive, and we are human and imperfect and sometimes do lie and/or deceive, as you did on Friday night [I had not been completely honest with my dad about who was going to the movies with me]. The irony is that, if you had fully disclosed everything, I would have allowed you to go to the movies; but since you didn't tell me the truth, and I found out that you lied, I grounded you.

Please try harder to say what you mean and mean what you say. The truth, no matter how bad, is better than any lie(s).

Be SMART!

Love, Dad

How honest are you? When have you told a lie to impress others? When have you lied to your parents or anyone else to cover up for yourself? Lying can become a habit and ruin your reputation. Have you ever read any of Shakespeare's plays? The futility of lying is often a subplot.

{ **Character** }

Dear Anthony,

There is a Jewish saying: "The man who has confidence in himself gains the confidence of others." A man who has confidence in himself never needs to put on airs. I have noticed of late an improvement in your level of self-confidence. I have especially noticed how well you have handled disappointment. That's a sign of fortitude, an important component of character. Keep it up.

Love, Dad

When have you shown fortitude? How did it affect your self-confidence? If it did not help your self-confidence, try to discern why. Have you fully recognized all your talents? If you have, are you using them? Happiness and self-confidence grow through activity, not idleness or watching TV. Choose to participate; fuel your mind, body, and soul.

{ **Self-Confidence** }

Dear Anthony,

I love to see you smile. Have you noticed when you have a smile on your face that people inevitably smile back at you? A smile is contagious, isn't it? It's tough to feel sad when you're smiling, so keep on smiling.

Love, Dad

How often is a smile on your face? Try to have a smile on your face all day long. It's good therapy. It keeps your attitude positive. It's difficult to be sad if you're smiling. Have some fun: Smile at people you don't know and watch their reactions.

{ **Happiness, Attitude** }

Dear Anthony,

You never need to worry about what people think of you because you are a young man of good character. Besides, you would be surprised at how infrequently people actually <u>do</u> think about others.

Love, Dad

Are you concerned about what people think of you? It's a needless worry. Instead, concern yourself with what *God* thinks of you. What is he thinking about you?

{ **Character, Self-Confidence** }

Dear Anthony,

Here are some additional thoughts on how to be a happy teen:

* Emulate positive adult role models.

* Have frequent dialogues with your family and friends.

* Play hard, work hard, love hard, pray hard, and go to church.

* Count your blessings and remember to thank God daily.

* Be choosy about whom you date.

* Avoid pitfalls like persons, places, or things that can be physically or spiritually harmful.

Be SMART!

Love, Dad

How many of the items on this list do you practice? How happy are you? If you have been properly reflecting on the comments and journaling your thoughts, you should be developing self-confidence and a strong character. Are you? If you haven't started making changes yet, remember that only you can direct your life the way you want it to go.

{ **Happiness, Character** }

Dear Anthony,

Sirach, one of the great prophets of the Old Testament, said: "May your soul rejoice in God's mercy, and may you never be ashamed to praise him" (Sirach 51:29 NRSV). Jesus echoed these words, reminding us to never be ashamed of him or he will be ashamed of us. That's why we say grace before a meal, even in public.

Love, Dad

How do you cherish your faith? How do you love Jesus? Don't be afraid to show your love for Jesus. Sing it to the mountaintops, and in your neighborhood, too. You can "shout very loudly" by simply imitating Jesus.

{ Faith }

Dear Anthony,

The highest value we Americans have is the freedom to choose, provided it does not infringe on the freedom or rights of others. Ironically, this doesn't seem to apply to birth and death in our society, as we have seen with the horrors and tragedies of abortion and euthanasia.

Pope John Paul II has called our society a "culture of death." The pope is also referring to the death penalty. In all three cases, a life is taken—a life created by God.

It is our responsibility to help right these wrongs by praying and speaking out when it is appropriate to do so.

Love, Dad

What do you think about the sanctity of life? Do you think that there is ever a time when death should be a choice? The sanctity of life is the basis of all moral teaching in the church. What does that mean to you?

{ **Faith, Character** }

Dear Anthony,

We live in what Ronald Reagan called a "Teflon society," a society where people shirk responsibility. They act as if the Ten Commandments and the teachings and values of Jesus Christ are nothing more than suggestions.

If you haven't already, you will soon encounter these types of individuals, especially when you enter college. Be steadfast in your beliefs, Son. There are many "voices" out there clamoring for your attention and "defection."

Be SMART!

Love, Dad

How do you take responsibility for your actions? How do some people shirk their responsibilities? The life of the Christian should always mirror the life of Jesus. It is challenging and even difficult, yet there is intense joy for those who take the risk to live as Christians. Remember, if you're challenged, refer to WWJD, and take heart.

{ Character, Responsibility }

Dear Anthony,

When God created man he used the plural: "Let us create." It was the first of his reminders that God meant God the Father, God the Son, and God the Holy Spirit. We are reminded of the Holy Trinity each time we bless ourselves.

I mention this because soon you will be receiving confirmation, the last sacrament of initiation, and as the apostles did on Pentecost, you, too, will receive the Holy Spirit.

Much like your Jewish friends who have been called to their bar mitzvah, you will now be considered an adult and a fully initiated Catholic.

Love, Dad

Have you ever felt the Holy Spirit acting through you? What do you think it feels like? The Holy Spirit gives us the zeal to act as a true witness of Christ and the ability to live out our faith despite the consequences we may encounter. Ask the Holy Spirit for inspiration and the words to defend your faith whenever it is challenged.

{ Faith }

195

Dear Anthony,

A follow—up on the role of the Holy Spirit:

It was the Holy Spirit who gave Jesus human life through the Blessed Virgin Mary. It was the Holy Spirit who empowered Jesus during his temptation. He gives us gifts/strength in teaching, witnessing, and serving. St. Paul tells us the Spirit of God comes to fill our human nature so that "It is not I who live, but Christ in me."

I hope by now you've noted the special connection between the Holy Spirit and the sacrament of confirmation.

Love, Dad

What gifts has the Holy Spirit given you? How are you using them? Remember, your talents grow when you use them and deteriorate when you don't use them.

{ **Faith, Stewardship** }

Dear Anthony,

You are very good at accomplishing your goals but are sometimes neglectful in doing your chores. Allow me to paraphrase Helen Keller, who said she longed to accomplish noble things, but knew it was her chief duty to accomplish humble tasks, as though they were great and noble.

Please try harder to remember all your chores.

Be SMART!

Love, Dad

What chores do you have to do each week? Do you procrastinate when it comes to doing them or try to get away with not doing them at all? Why? Neglectfulness could become a bad habit. How can you best follow the example of Helen Keller?

{ **Responsibility** }

Dear Anthony,

Like your football exercises, spirituality involves a regimen as well. Here is a synopsis of the standard established by St. Ignatius Loyola, the founder of the Jesuits:

* We must always acknowledge our sinfulness before God and accept his mercy.

* We must establish a regimen of prayer.

* We must meditate on Christ's passion.

* We must meditate on the glory of the Resurrection.

For St. Ignatius, seeking God in all things is at the center of spiritual life.

Love, Dad

What do you think of St. Ignatius's regimen? Could you follow it? A good spirituality is the key to short, long, and eternal happiness. God wishes for all of us to be happy, and through St. Ignatius Loyola, he has given us an effective formula for happiness. Is there any reason not to follow these simple steps?

{ Faith }

Dear Anthony,

Congratulations on being confirmed
by Bishop Curry this past Saturday!
Remember his words of wisdom about
taking responsibility for your life and the
lives of others.

Mom and I are very proud of you, and
hope you do get your wish to become a
confirmation team leader.

Love, Dad

Continuing to learn about our faith and passing it on to others is an obligation placed on us by Jesus. In what ways can you deepen your faith and pass it on to others? Did you realize that the apostles and St. Paul passed their faith on to new believers, who, in turn, did the same. This process has been going on for nearly two thousand years and will continue until the end of time.

{ Faith }

Dear Anthony,

Having a girlfriend places additional responsibilities upon you where your existing friends are concerned. You can never take them for granted and assume that they will always be there when you're ready to spend time with them. Your friends have become part of who you are, and the only way to maintain a relationship with them is by spending time with them and letting them know how important they are to you.

Love, Dad

Do you take your friends for granted? Every relationship requires communication in order to remain healthy. What steps can you take to ensure your friendships will be long-lasting?

_____

_____

_____

_____

_____

_____

_____

_____

_____

_____

_____

_____

_____

_____

_____

_____

_____

_____

_____

{ **Friendship** }

Dear Anthony,

It's great that you and Matt have remained such close friends. I consider him an excellent role model. Notice the pride and sincerity he shows for his Jewish faith, by going from Reform to Orthodox. [Reform is the most "liberal" branch of Judaism; Orthodox, the most "conservative," and the most devout.] He may be the only one amongst his friends, but his virtue keeps him from fearing criticism or being made fun of.

Love, Dad

How do you deal with people who may seem strange to you because of their race, culture, or religion? We are all children of God. We should seek to see God in others.

Do you live your faith publicly, or do you try to keep it a secret from others? Remember what Jesus said: "If you are ashamed of me, I will be ashamed of you."

{ **Faith, Respect** }

Dear Anthony,

Always follow your conscience rather than conform to the opinions of others or try to impress them. As Shakespeare wrote: "To thine own self be true." You're a wonderful young man and people should accept you as you are, not as they want you to be.

Be SMART!

Love, Dad

How are you true to yourself? Do you ever try to impress others by being something you're not? Why or why not? Trying to impress others could be an indication of low self-confidence. Review and implement those things that can help you improve your self-esteem.

{ **Character, Self-Confidence** }

Dear Anthony,

Mahatma Gandhi said that seven things will kill us:

* getting something through nefarious means

* a lack of responsibility and accountability

* a misuse of knowledge

* a lack of ethics

* a mentality which has at its core "progress at any cost"

* the social facade of religion/using religion to justify evil

* a lack of moral leadership

The antidote to these seven things is a strong value system.

Be SMART!

Love, Dad

210

What we're really talking about is having strong moral character. What additional steps can you take to strengthen your character? By now you should already have made great strides in building up your character. If not, do so. You owe it to yourself and the Lord.

{ Character }

Dear Anthony,

As you approach the end of the semester, I thought it would be appropriate to share with you a thought from the British historian Arnold Toynbee. He defined <u>life</u> as a voyage of discovery, not a safe harbor.

It's similar to the thought I have shared with you about being bold and aggressive, and seizing opportunities as they come along.

Love, Dad

What opportunities have you passed on? Why? We grow physically, mentally, and spiritually by taking action, not by being a bystander. Why do others succeed? Do you think they are just lucky? The truth is they are taking advantage of opportunity. Be assured, you can succeed as well.

Like "the little engine that could," remember the words: *I think I can.*

{ Success }

Dear Anthony,

The painting of George Washington kneeling in prayer in the snow is one of the most famous in American history. In this picture, Washington personifies those people who recognize that it's not enough to depend solely on their own courage or goodness, but that God must figure prominently in their lives.

We honor that recognition through prayer.

Did you know that the first Continental Congress started the practice of beginning each meeting with a prayer, or that Ben Franklin rose to invoke the Almighty as the Constitution was being drafted?

Love, Dad

The fact that even our greatest heroes recognize the need for God to be at the center of their lives should encourage you to develop a good prayer life. What steps can you take to develop a daily regimen of prayer?

_____

_____

_____

_____

_____

_____

_____

_____

_____

_____

_____

_____

_____

_____

_____

_____

_____

_____

{ Prayer }

Dear Anthony,

Jesus lived a life full of purpose, with purpose, on purpose. His purpose was our redemption, and every action and every word he spoke witnessed to that purpose.

Purpose isn't a goal; it's more like a direction. It is something that you never achieve, but rather it is fulfilled in every moment that you are "on" purpose. Purpose defines the course that you will take in life.

Love, Dad

What is your purpose in life? Perhaps you are unsure what *purpose* is. Here are some examples of defined purposes: *to love and serve God by loving and serving others* or *to impact the lives of other people in a positive way.* What, then, will your purpose be?

{ **Stewardship** }

Dear Anthony,

This is finals week in the NBA and at Agoura High School. We can certainly tell that both the Pistons and the Lakers prepared well for the finals. You should prepare well by making studying your number one priority and avoiding unnecessary distractions. Then remember to "do what you are doing."

Love, Dad

Remember the Boy Scout motto: "Be prepared." There is nothing that can be done well without proper preparation. What are some ways you can improve your study habits?

{ Studying }

Dear Anthony,

As the semester comes to a close, I want to focus on motivation.

I've always told you that one major key to success is our ability to communicate. Successful businessmen and other professionals communicate better because they have larger vocabularies. Imagine if you learned one word every day. What would the size of your vocabulary be six years from now when you graduate from college?

Love, Dad

How well do speak and write? What efforts are you willing to make to improve your speaking and writing ability? This is an investment in yourself that you need to make if you desire to succeed in life.

{ **Communication, Success** }

Dear Anthony,

Another key to success is how we deliver our message. In other words, how you say what you say. For instance, Ronald Reagan, who was known as "the great communicator," always delivered his message with obvious sincerity and self-confidence. He mostly smiled during his speeches, but, when necessary, would appear very stern. He exuded self-confidence, and as a result, was a strong leader.

Ronald Reagan understood that people remember only about 20 percent of what is said and about 80 percent of how it is said. What that means is that there is no room for banal or insipid speech in effective communication. Start preparing now for your victory speech.

Love, Dad

How comfortable are you speaking in public? What is your greatest fear about speaking to a group of people? To become an effective speaker requires time and patience, but it is well worth the effort. Are you willing to invest a little time in yourself? You can begin by reading dialogue in front of a mirror, with a cassette recorder nearby to tape your voice. Practice changing your facial expressions when appropriate, and later, listen to your voice. Practice, practice, practice.

{ **Communication, Self-Confidence** }

Dear Anthony,

Congratulations on completing your sophomore year. Great job! I hope we get to do a lot of things together this summer.

Through the notes that I've tossed into your lunch bags this year, I gave you advice on how to get along with friends, how to seize each day, how to feel good about yourself, how important family time is, how to make sound moral decisions, how to communicate effectively, how important it is to maintain a positive attitude, and several other topics as well.

It can be best summed up as: "Be all you can be," and live a life pleasing to God.

Love, Dad

What did you learn about yourself that you did not know before reading *More Lunch Bag Notes?*

We hope that you discovered how wonderful you are, and how dear you are to your parents, to your friends, and to God.

Remember, no one on the earth can make you feel inferior without your permission. Be SMART and boldly go places you've never gone before.

Index of Themes

Action, 26–27, 34–35

Attitude, 24–25, 32–33, 62–63, 82–83, 84–85, 120–21, 128–29, 182–83

Character, 22–23, 46–47, 58–59, 74–75, 100–1, 116–17, 124–25, 126–27, 132–33, 134–35, 160–61, 178–79, 184–85, 186–87, 190–91, 192–93, 208–9, 210–11

Choices, 2–3, 22–23, 92–93, 134–35, 146–47, 160–61

Communication, 102–3, 130–31, 220–21, 222–23

Dating, 8–9, 96–97, 130–31, 174–75

Failure, 36–37, 48–49, 68–69, 106–7, 114–15, 118–19, 120–21

Faith, 72–73, 78–79, 88–89, 94–95, 114–15, 138–39, 142–43, 144–45, 164–65, 170–71, 172–73, 188–89, 190–91, 194–95, 196–97, 200–1, 202–3, 206–7

Family, 20–21, 54–55, 56–57, 70–71, 80–81, 104–5, 122–23

Forgiveness, 98–99, 166–67, 176–77

Friendship, 10–11, 38–39, 56–57, 176–77, 204–5

Gratitude, 42–43, 78–79, 108–9

Happiness, 34–35, 40–41, 58–59, 106–7, 112–13, 156–57, 182–83, 186–87

Prayer, 144–45, 158–59, 214–15

Priorities, 150–51, 152–53, 162–63

Respect, 18–19, 50–51, 56–57, 64–65, 100–1, 206–7

Responsibility, 28–29, 76–77, 148–49, 192–93, 198–99

Self-Confidence, 4–5, 52–53, 136–37, 154–55, 180–81, 184–85, 208–9, 222–23

Stewardship, 20–21, 30–31, 40–41, 140–41, 168–69, 172–73, 196–97, 216–17

Index of Themes

Studying, 6–7, 12–13, 14–15, 60–61, 218–19

Success, 12–13, 16–17, 44–45, 66–67, 68–69, 70–71, 82–83, 86–87, 90–91, 110–11, 118–19, 212–13, 220–21

What Did You Think?

Teenagers, we would like to hear from you. Let us know how *More Lunch Bag Notes* has affected you. Tell us which notes were the most meaningful to you and why. Send us the personal affirmations that you have written.

Parents, we invite you to share your thoughts as well. Are you writing lunch bag notes yourself, or have you developed another unique way to communicate with your kids? Do you have a favorite note that you've written and would like to share? If so, we would love to hear about it. We might even collect the best ones in a future anthology.

Please mail any correspondence to:

Anthony and Al Parisi
P.O. Box 1365
Agoura Hills, CA 91376

Join In. Speak Up. Help Out!

Would you like to help Loyola Press improve our publications? Become one of our special Loyola Press Advisors. From time to time, registered advisors will be invited to participate in brief online surveys. We will recognize your efforts with various gift certificates, points, and prizes. For more information, visit www.SpiritedTalk.org.